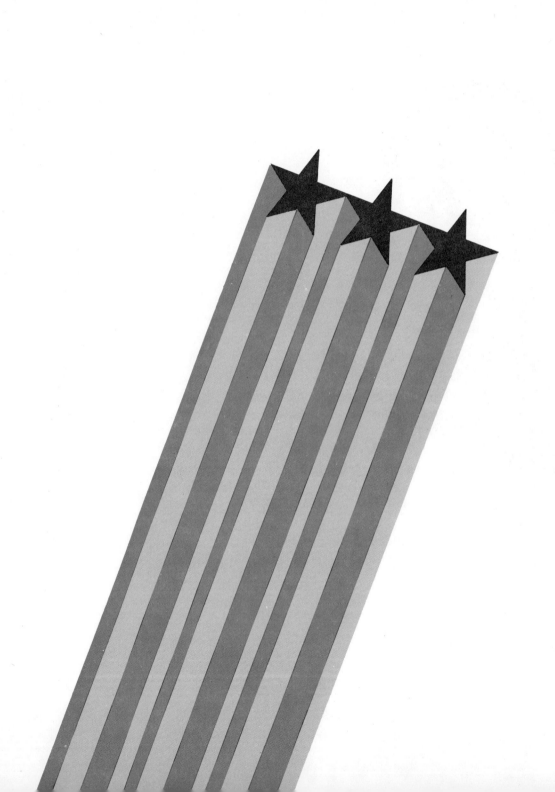

Sonny&Cher

by Thomas Braun
designed by Mark Landkamer

CREATIVE EDUCATION
CHILDRENS PRESS

Published by Creative Education, Inc., 123 South Broad Street, Mankato, Minnesota 56001 Copyright © 1978 by Creative Education, Inc. International copyrights reserved in all countries. No part of this book may be reproduced in any form without written permission from the publisher. Printed in the United States.

Library of Congress Cataloging in Publication Data

Braun, Thomas, 1944-
  Sonny and Cher.

  SUMMARY: Relates the rise from poverty to television stardom of singers Sonny and Cher.
  1. Bono, Sonny — Juvenile literature. 2. Cher, 1946-   — Juvenile literature. 3. Singers — United States — Biography — Juvenile literature. [1. Bono, Sonny. 2. Cher, 1946-   3. Singers] I. Title.
ML3930.B593B7   784'.092'2 [B] [920] 77-24706
ISBN 0-87191-620-7

Photographs:

Sunday night television offers viewers a real choice. There's Walt Disney, of course. For most people there's always been Disney. Bears, wolves, cougars, antelope — sometimes even real people — get themselves and their friends caught in tight spots. But it's never very serious and everything always works out for the best.

Then there's the show about the man worth six million dollars. Part human and rest wires, gears and other fancy hardware. His name is Steve Austin. He's "bionic" which means he can run faster, jump higher and see farther than any of his weekly enemies. Steve also has a bionic friend, Jamey Sommers, who has her own TV series and often appears with Colonel Austin.

Together Steve and Jamey make an extraordinary couple. But there's another TV couple whose on and off-stage adventures have involved more conflicts and triumphs than the bionic pair could ever imagine. Sonny and Cher have never had to outrun a train or wrestle with Bigfoot, yet their accomplishments both together and separately have taken just as much energy and have demonstrated much greater talents.

There are several ways to get to know Sonny and Cher. A good place to start is to watch them working together on Sunday night.

Sunday Night

"The Sonny and Cher Show" opens with all the appropriate glitter and applause of a prime-time variety show. The announcer lists the special guests for the evening. The audience, sitting close to the small stage, looks and sounds eager. And the classic rock

"The Sonny and Cher Show"

7

theme—"And the Beat Goes On"—goes on, gathering everyone's attention.

Sonny and Cher make their entrance with a song. It's always a familiar number, either one of their own hits or some other popular tune arranged to fit their musical style. They perform easily together, creating a distinctive kind of harmony. At the same time they give the impression of being two very different people. One seems so unlike the other.

In terms of physical appearance, they look as different as Laurel and Hardy. Everything about Cher is long and narrow—face, body, hair, even her fingernails. Everything about Sonny is short and round. She wears clothes that celebrate her grace and beauty. He often looks uncomfortable in his bow tie and tuxedo.

As the opening musical number ends, Sonny and Cher switch from music to comedy. Suddenly it becomes obvious that their success as entertainers has grown, not in spite of their differences, but because of them. Their comedy comes out of a playful kind of personal combat. They attack and retreat and attack again, but always just for the fun of it.

It usually goes something like this:

Sonny might begin with a simple compliment, "That's a pretty dress you have on."

"Thank you."

"Ya know Cher," Sonny says with a grin, for the moment feeling very much in command of the situation, "I just finished a book. . ."

"You mean you're done with your new coloring book already?" The audience laughs. Cher's interruption clearly signals the start of another battle of insults. Sonny nods and laughs along with the audience.

"Aw Cher, you're so quick."

"Aw Sonny, you're so short." More laughter. Cher has done it to him again and Sonny knows it. He's losing the battle. In a situation like this he usually switches tactics and makes an appeal for sympathy.

"All right, Cher. That's O.K. I don't mind being put down like that. Really. I came out here feeling good. . .tried to start an interesting conversation and right away you hit me with a couple of cheap little shots. . ."

Cher jumps in, "Speaking of cheap little shots, what do you hear from your mother?"

And the comedy goes on. Cher usually wins with a few well-aimed words. Sonny usually loses, trying to set traps for Cher but always falling into them himself.

Many of their comic exchanges make fun of some of the serious conflicts that Sonny and Cher have struggled through and resolved during their long career. At the end of a recent show, they made their regular appearance on stage together. They had just finished a funny routine about a familiar TV soap opera.

"Ya know, Cher," Sonny said, "if we ever stopped doing this show, we could probably do a soap opera."

"Sonny, we are a soap opera." Cher's reply got a laugh from the audience, but is was a knowing laugh. Most of their fans know that the couple's off-stage life together has often been more complicated than any day-time TV melodrama. From the start their lives seemed to be part of a plot created by a Hollywood scriptwriter.

One of Sonny's earliest memories is of being hungry; not hunger for attention or success, but the more basic kind of hunger caused by a lack of food. Sonny's real name is Salvatore Bono. He was born on February 16, 1935 in Detroit, Michigan. His parents, Santo and Jean Bono, had immigrated to the United States from Sicily, and like many newcomers to America during that period, their struggle for survival was difficult.

When Sonny was seven years old he and his family moved from Detroit to Los Angeles. There his father worked on the Douglas Aircraft assembly line. By the time Sonny was old enough to enter Inglewood Union High School his parents were divorced. Sonny had to help support himself by working at odd jobs. He was a waiter, construction worker, masseur, butcher's helper and a truck driver.

One of his early jobs was at a grocery store. He had always been interested in music and by this time had tried writing a few songs. One afternoon at the grocery store he was unpacking a box of Koko Joe Cookies. Sonny like the sound of the brand-name and wrote a song called "Koko Joe." Several years later the song was recorded by the Righteous Brothers.

Sonny wrote other songs and spent most of his off-hours trying to sell them to local recording companies. Specialty Records bought his tune, "High School Dance," and hired him as an assistant producer. At his new job Sonny worked with Sam Cooke, Little Richard and several other top recording stars.

After a brief unsuccessful attempt to start his own record company, Sonny went to work for Phil Spector at Philles Records. He continued writing songs including "You Bug Me, Baby" and "Needles and Pins," and all

Salvatore

11

the while Sonny gained important experience in the music business. He learned about sound engineering, arranging and even stepped in to sing background music for the Crystals, the Ronettes, and the Righteous Brothers. Although Sonny had never been a good student in high school and had dropped out before graduation, he was receiving the best education the record industry could offer.

Cherilyn

Cherilyn Sarkisian was born in El Centro, California on May 20, 1946. Like Sonny, Cher has a clear memory of poverty. She remembers walking to school wearing shoes held together with rubber bands. At home the question asked most frequently was "How are we going to pay the rent?" Another problem for Cher was her mother's long series of marriages. Her mother has been married eight times. Three of those times she married John Sarkisian, Cher's father.

Early in her life, Cher, her mother and her half-sister, Georgeanne moved to Los Angeles. Cher's mother, Georgia, worked as a fashion model, an actress in commercials and came close to starting a career in the movies. She was cast in the film, "The Asphalt Jungle." But at the last minute the part was taken away from Georgia and given to another aspiring actress, Marilyn Monroe.

The constant changes in her life left Cher unhappy and insecure. "I was a shy, ugly kid who led a big fantasy life," she recalls. "When I was little, my mom and I used to go to Hollywood Boulevard and buy a couple of hot dogs and sit in our car watching the interesting people go by."

12

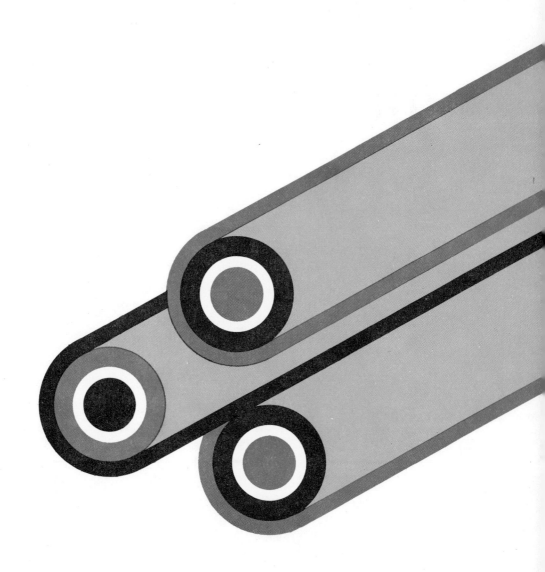

Along with the hot dogs, Cher had the typical Hollywood dream: "I grew up thinking I wanted to be a movie star, because they were happy; they wore diamonds. That kind of life would take me away from all that was real and ugly. I always felt really embarrassed about being poor because I though it was punishment for something I had done wrong."

Cher had a natural musical talent. "From the time I could talk," she says, "I began to sing. Singing just came from the inside—something I'd do without thinking whenever I felt good or was really blue." But a musical career wasn't her first choice. She dropped out of Montclair High School during her junior year, left home and began taking acting lessons.

Caesar and Cleo

Sonny and Cher met for the first time on a double-date. "I was knocked out," Cher remembers. "I didn't think he was handsome, but I'd never seen anyone with long hair and boots and stuff like that...But there was something about him. He was good, stable, older—sweet."

It didn't take long for Sonny to discover Cher's singing ability. He said, "In the first two weeks I knew her, I told her I felt she would be a great star." He convinced her to give up her acting ambitions and concentrate instead on developing her voice.

Soon after they met, Sonny took Cher to observe a recording session at Philles Records. There she was introduced to Phil Spector. Cher was overwhelmed by Spector's genius and the complexity of the process that created the famous "Spector sound." The brilliant young

14

producer carefully supervised every step of the recording procedure. For many of his records he wrote both the music and the lyrics himself. He selected the singers, made fine adjustments on the musical instruments and personally operated most of the sound equipment. Clearly Spector was a perfectionist. A two or three minute single record took hours, often days of hard work before Spector was satisfied with the results.

On one of her visits to the studio, Cher was given a chance to do more than just watch the busy proceedings. When one of the background singers failed to show up, an assistant noticed Cher standing on the sidelines and asked her if she could sing. Cher said, "No." But the assistant was desperate. "Well, can you carry a tune?" he asked. Cher said she could and suddenly she was doing background music for a record by the Crystals. From that time on she became an active regular at the sessions.

Sonny tried to persuade Phil Spector to let his new girlfriend make a record of her own. Spector agreed, but Cher's first attempt was unsuccessful. Then Sonny and Cher decided to try performing together. They adopted the stage names, Caesar and Cleo, and worked briefly at a small night club called the Purple Onion. They also cut their first single record together. The song was "The Letter" and, like Cher's first attempt, it was a flop.

Despite their early failures, Sonny and Cher were not easily discouraged. They were drawn together by their fierce ambition to make it big in show business. As a young girl Cher had survived by building her own fantasies of becoming a star. Now with Sonny's talent for song writing and his inside knowledge of the record

business, Cher's own vision of stardom seemed clearer than ever. Frequently the couple drove into the foothills outside of Los Angeles and parked in front of a 31-room mansion owned by Tony Curtis. Staring through the huge iron gates, they vowed to each other that someday the mansion would belong to them.

Before long they decided to take another trip and exchange a different kind of vow. On October 27, 1964, they drove south, crossed the border into Mexico and were married in Tijuana.

"I Got You Babe"

Sonny and Cher struggled toward success at a time when popular music was undergoing one of its frequent revolutions.

The most significant musical style of the 1950s was, of course, rock and roll. The new music grew into a kind of national anthem for youth. The new national heroes had names like Paul Anka, Pat Boone, Elvis, Buddy Holly, Chuck Berry, the Everly Brothers and the Platters. Their music—"At the Hop," "Teen Angel," "Sweet Little Sixteen," "Wake Up Little Susie"—celebrated the frantic, romantic world of teenagers. There were songs about dances and drive-ins, but most of the lyrics told about the wonderful misery of boys and girls falling in and out of love.

Teenagers bought records, listened to the Top Forty on radio and watched their favorite counterparts dancing close on TV's "American Bandstand." And they moved into the 1960 doing "The Twist" at places called "discotheques."

While a large segment of the youth population was listening to "Be Bop Baby" and "Bye-Bye Love," a smaller, but just as enthusiastic group was discovering folk music. There was really nothing new about the music itself. The traditions of folk music were, in fact, very long and old. Previously this simple music was confined to remote geographical regions. Then along came Pete Seeger, The Kingston Trio, Joan Baez and Peter, Paul and Mary. They recorded the classic folk ballads and rapidly attracted a national audience.

The most creative and influential performer in the new folk wave was Bob Dylan. His first album, "Bob Dylan," came out in 1962 and was followed a year later with "The Freewheelin' Bob Dylan." His music was very different from rock and roll. His sound was rough, even harsh. While the rock hits tended to be repetitious and hypnotic, Dylan demanded the attention of his listeners. The almost irritating quality of his voice forced his audience to listen to his words. His early songs contained urgent messages about the world, about human problems, social issues, war, and prejudice. He was a musical folk-poet writing and singing about real concerns.

Rock and roll and Bob Dylan dominated the musical scene of the early 1960s. Most young people had a distinct preference for either one type of music or the other, either rock or folk. Most older people had a distinct preference for neither one. Then something happened to blur all of the distinctions. The Beatles arrived. The music of John, Paul, George and Ringo was related to the rock sound, yet they were bigger than single tradition. They couldn't be easily classified. They were just the Beatles.

As Sonny and Cher moved closer to their first big record, another trend was developing in popular music. The new sound merged the big beat of rock and roll with the message-quality of Bob Dylan. The style was called folk-rock, and one of the first groups to popularize the new music was The Byrds. Early in 1965, The Byrds took Dylan's song, "Mr. Tambourine Man," added electric guitars and came up with a folk-rock classic.

When Sonny and Cher's time came, it came very fast. It came in the midst of the folk-rock revolution.

Their first moderately successful record, "Baby Don't Go," was released in the spring of 1965. Written by Sonny, the song has a mournful, slow-pounding beat punctuated by a lone harmonica. Cher does the main lyrics alone and Sonny joins her for the refrain. The piece tells a simple story about an 18-year-old girl who decides she must move away from the small town in which she has spent her entire life. She must leave her boyfriend and flee to the city where she will "be a lady someday." Cher sings about loneliness, poverty and a vague hope of finding a new home and a happier life. The boy-girl theme so popular in the old rock hits is present in "Baby Don't Go." But a new sense of alienation has been added and becomes the dominant mood. Perhaps the song draws its message about isolation from Cher's own troubled past.

Sonny and Cher's next record and their first real smash hit was "I Got You Babe," released in June, 1965. The lyrics of this song leave no doubt that Sonny and Cher are making a very personal musical statement about themselves, about how they see themselves and how others see them.

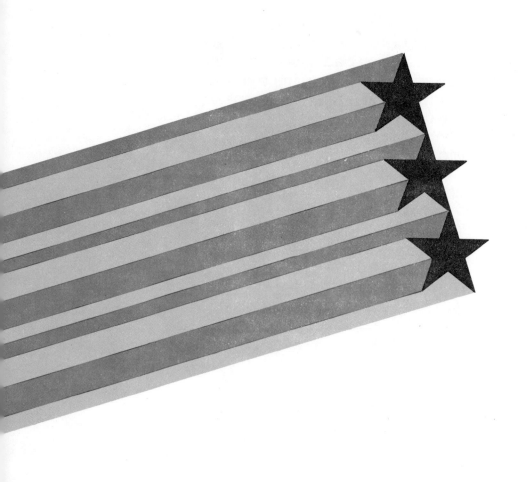

They carry on a singing dialogue with each other. Again, Cher expresses feelings of alienation from a society critical of youthful ways. She lists the criticisms: "They say we're young and we don't know," "They say our love won't pay the rent," "So let them say your hair's too long." But in the face of this social disapproval they find mutual security and strength by just being together. Sonny tells Cher, "Well, I don't know if all that's true, 'cause you got me and baby I got you, babe. . ."

Someone listening to "I Got You Babe" may find the lyrics no different from the shallow love themes of "Tears On My Pillow" or "Teenager in Love." But there are differences. There is a new kind of protest in their songs that the older music didn't have. Another difference concerns Sonny and Cher's personal involvement in their music. During this period, Sonny and Cher, like the Beatles, were larger than their music. They were more than just singers. Along with making music they were creating a highly visible public image of themselves. They were personalities supposedly living the kind of life and confronting the kinds of problems expressed in their songs.

Their physical appearance was an extremely important part of their total impact. Their hair—Sonny's long, Cher's longer—and their dress—Sonny's bobcat vest and moccasins, Cher's bell-bottom pants —became symbols of their protest and nonconformity.

On their first tour of England they were thrown out of London's Hilton Hotel because of the way they dressed. "I had on one of my pride-and-joy outfits," Cher recalls. "It was red, white and blue stripped bell-bottoms with an industrial zipper with a ring on it. And a top with big bell sleeves, and a pair of red shoes. And Sonny had on

a pair of striped pants and his dress Eskimo boots, real beautiful." Today these outfits would seem commonplace, but in the mid-1960s they were considered "cool" by some and outrageous by others.

Sonny and Cher's early hits are not only different from the older rock favorites, but their music is also distinct from the songs written and performed by Bob Dylan. The differences are most obvious in a comparison of "I Got You Babe" and Dylan's "It Ain't Me, Babe." The titles alone suggest the contrast. Sonny and Cher declare their togetherness . Their love for each other will prevail over any opposition. Whatever goes wrong, they still have each other. Dylan's statement is just the opposite. It is a declaration of independence. He doesn't want to be the one "who'll pick you up each time you fall." The quality of Dylan's protest is much deeper and more severe than Sonny and Cher's.

By the end of September, 1965, Sonny and Cher had achieved a rare distinction. Five of their single records—"I Got You Babe," "All I Really Want to Do," "Just You," "Laugh at Me," and "Baby Don't Go"— appeared on the hit charts at the same time. In less than six months they had risen to the top of the music world.

"Good Times" and Bad

For two years following the explosive start of their recording career, Sonny and Cher enjoyed their roles as pop super-heroes. They toured the United States and Europe, giving live concerts. Every show was a sell-out. Their fans received each appearance with wild enthusiasm, sometimes hysteria. People fought to get close enough to touch them. Once, at Los Angeles airport, the couple was nearly swallowed up by a mob of 10,000 screaming teenagers.

Sonny and Cher began to look for other ways to express their creative energies. Cher started designing clothes and marketing the styles that she and Sonny had made so popular. Sonny wrote the music and conducted the orchestra for the movie, "Good Times," in which he and Cher took the leading roles.

The film shows the couple playing themselves. They sing, show off their wild costumes and display the easy fun of being happily married singing stars. One critic wrote that the movie is a "colorful, sprightly bit of good-humored silliness." Another film reviewer described Sonny and Cher as "an ingratiating couple, he, long-haired and comic in a way that recalls Harpo Marx and the Three Stooges; she, long-haired and attractive and robustly voiced, fine for the songs which are bright and brassy."

By the end of 1967, Sonny and Cher's records had sold over 40 million copies. Then, just as suddenly as their wave of popularity had arrived, it began an abrupt decline. The folk-rock trend disappeared, another musical fashion took its place and Sonny and Cher weren't able to keep up with the change.

The shift in musical taste signaled the arrival of a whole new youth culture. The participants in the new culture called themselves "hippies." They promoted a simple life-style based on freedom, love and "flower power." They opposed the war in Viet Nam, resisted the draft and experimented with psychedelic drugs, particularly LSD or "acid." Their music, sometimes referred to as "acid rock" or "hard rock," became the chief symbol of the movement. The groups that made

U. S. 1991047

the music had names like Jefferson Airplane, The Doors, The Grateful Dead and The Mothers of Invention.

Sonny and Cher not only couldn't keep up with the changes in the music scene, but they didn't want to. "The whole sound and style of music began to come out of the drug culture," Sonny observed. "We didn't want to get into that, so it left us." In fact, the couple had such strong feelings about the use of drugs that they made an anti-marijuana film. The movie was distributed to high schools as part of a government drug education campaign.

Having been abandoned by their teenage audience, Sonny and Cher decided to try their luck at the movies again. Sonny wrote, directed and produced "Chastity." "I wanted to do the film so badly," Sonny has said. "I raised all my own money for it — putting my house in hock in order to do it."

In the film Cher plays the part of a young runaway girl trying to establish her own identity and a sense of independence. Most critics agreed that Chastity was a bomb. The kindest statement made by one critic was that "Cher has a marvelous quality that often makes you forget the lines you are hearing."

By 1969 their career in show business had collapsed. And worse, Sonny and Cher were broke.

Dreams don't just fade away. Sonny and Cher were determined not to accept their decline and quietly disappear from show business forever. Instead, they looked closely at their situation and tried to learn something from it.

TV

"The biggest mistake a performer makes is to try to stay a teenager," Sonny said. "Young kids have a new idol every year. Someone will always take your place." Sonny also felt that staying on top in the record business was too demanding. "Getting a hit record constantly was on my mind. It gave you three more months of survival as a star. It was almost like a probationary period. When three months were up, the panic was on. . .I don't want to be in that position again."

The couple realized that, in order to survive as entertainers, they needed to change their appeal and develop a new audience. They decided to launch their comeback effort on the nightclub circuit. They soon found that life on the road wasn't easy. At first their audiences were small, sometimes they played to less than 50 people. But they continued to travel back and forth across the country performing a hectic series of one-night stands.

Slowly they began to create and perfect a style more suitable for adult audiences. Their act included a few of their old folk-rock hits, but they also inserted some popular standards. One critic, taking note of this change, observed that "the couple has matured into such sensitive interpreters that they can transform even the most overfamiliar material into searingly soulful expressions, as witness Cher's fiery treatment of 'Danny Boy.' Truly Cher has developed into one of our most inspiring ladies of song."

Another important new addition to their act was comedy. They found that their audiences not only enjoyed their music, but they also appreciated their humor. The jokes came easily. Sonny played the naive straight-man always setting himself up for one of Cher's icy put-downs.

Soon Sonny and Cher were being booked into the best nightclubs in New York, Chicago, Los Angeles and Las Vegas. They also began making guest appearances on television. Early in 1971 Sonny and Cher were the guest-hosts on "The Merv Griffin Show." Fred Silverman, the programming director for CBS, happened to see their appearance and was immediately impressed by the couple's varied talents. At the time, CBS was looking for someone to do a six-week summer replacement series. Silverman offered the job to Sonny and Cher and within a few months "The Sonny and Cher Comedy Hour" made its television debut. The one-hour variety show was so successful that CBS decided to make it a permanent part of its schedule.

The show's format has stayed about the same since it began in 1971. The couple sings, swaps insults and takes part in elaborately costumed comedy skits. Each week special guest stars join in the fun. The couple's favorite guest has always been their daughter Chastity.

Along with creating a hit television series, Sonny and Cher continued to make record albums and concert appearances. They were on top once more,

and this time they made it because of their own talents. They were no longer captives of a shifting musical trend. To celebrate their new-found security, they bought the 31-room mansion that, years before, had only been part of a remote dream.

Cher and Sonny

Inside their huge new home, Sonny and Cher surrounded themselves with all the usual symbols of wealth and stardom. They bought expensive antiques, hired servants and lined up six new cars in their garage. Many of their rooms were stuffed with new clothes. Once, in a single week, Cher spent 10,000 dollars to expand her already enormous wardrobe. Still, all of their wealth and professional security could not prevent another change from taking place.

For years they had worked to promote their public image. Their success as a married couple had always been measured in terms of their success as performers. Sonny and Cher's previous career struggles had kept them together but, at the same time, had made them extremely dependent on each other. They had never taken the time to stand back and consider their identities as individuals. When they eventually made the effort to look closely at their personal relationship, both found it unsatisfactory. As "The Sonny and Cher Comedy Hour" was achieving it highest ratings on television, their private act together began to pull apart.

Sonny quietly separated from Cher in May, 1973. On February 19 the following year he filed a court petition asking for a legal separation. Eight days later Cher sued for divorce. Soon after their private troubles became public, CBS announced the cancellation of their television series.

Since that time both Sonny and Cher have talked openly about their problems. "We couldn't do anything without each other," Cher said. "It used to make me furious because no one ever thought of us alone. Sonny and Cher. We were like Siamese twins." And she added, "I wanted some experiences of my own." Sonny has expressed confusion about the painful matter. "Sure I managed her life for her, but as far as we both knew we were in full harmony over our lifestyle. I couldn't have been happier, and I thought Cher felt the same way."

Whatever the grounds were for their disagreements, they both agreed to end their partnership without bitterness. Separately, they tried to start new careers. Sonny signed a contract with ABC television and opened "The Sonny Comedy Hour" in the fall of 1974. But the show didn't last long. He returned to songwriting and also developed his own nightclub act.

During the same season, "The Cher Show" premiered on CBS. After taping one of her programs, Cher made a quick decision. She remembers that she "picked up the phone and tracked down Sonny, who was out doing one-nighters in Denver, and I said, 'Son, I've got this crazy idea. . .' " She suggested that they put aside their personal differences and work together again on a new series. The following season "The Sonny and Cher Show" returned to television.

Sonny and Cher have indeed led a kind of soap-opera life together. But in spite of all the changes and difficulties, their basic talent has remained constant. They continue to offer one of the best choices on Sunday night television.

DIANA ROSS   JACKSON FIVE
THE OSMONDS   CARLY SIMON
CHARLIE RICH   BOB DYLAN
ELTON JOHN   JOHN DENVER
CHICAGO   THE BEATLES
FRANK SINATRA   ELVIS PRESLEY
BARBRA STREISAND   JOHNNY CASH
OLIVIA NEWTON-JOHN   CHARLEY PRIDE
CAPTAIN AND TENNILLE ARETHA FRANKLIN
TONY ORLANDO   ROBERTA FLACK
BARRY MANILOW   STEVIE WONDER
DONNY AND MARIE   NEIL DIAMOND
SONNY AND CHER   CAROLE KING

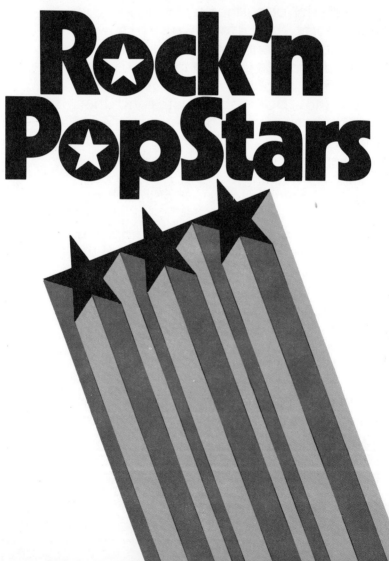